really easy piano

GW00457045

CHART HITS

VOLUME 2

WISE PUBLICATIONS
PART OF THE MUSIC SALES GROUP
LONDON / NEW YORK / PARIS / SYDNEY / COPENHAGEN / BERLIN / MADRID / HONG KONG / TOKYO

Adventure Of A Lifetime
Buckland/Champion/Martin/
Berryman/Hermansen/Eriksen
Universal Music Publishing MGB Limited/
EMI Music Publishing Ltd

Black Magic
Drewett/Michelsen/Erfjord/Purcell
Warner/Chappell Music Publishing Limited/
Kobalt Music Publishing Limited/Sony/
ATV Music Publishing Allegro (UK)

Eyes Shut
Thornton/Goldsworthy/Turkmen
Universal Music Publishing Limited

Hello
Adkins/Kurstin
EMI Music Publishing Ltd/
Universal Music Publishing Limited

History
Brunetta/Drewett/Ryan/Payne/Tomlinson
Universal/MCA Music Limited/Warner/
Chappell Music Publishing Limited/
BMG Rights Management (UK) Limited/PPM Music Ltd

Hold Back The River
Bay
Kobalt Music Publishing Limited

Hold My Hand
Wroldsen/Bennett/Glynne/Patterson
Reservoir/Reverb Music Ltd/
Universal Music Publishing Limited/
BMG Rights Management (UK) Limited/
EMI Music Publishing Ltd

Hymn For The Weekend
Berryman/Eriksen/Martin/Buckland/Champion/
Hermansen/Yard/Zant/Tovar
Reach Global Inc/
Universal Music Publishing MGB Limited/
EMI Music Publishing Ltd

I Really Like You
Svensson/Jepsen/Hindlin
Kobalt Music Publishing Limited/Universal/
MCA Music Limited

King
Smith/Thornton/Goldsworthy/
Turkmen/Ralph
Universal Music Publishing Limited/
Imagem Music/Sony/
ATV Music Publishing Allegro (UK)

Lay Me Down
Napier/Smith/Smith
Universal Music Publishing Limited/Sony/
ATV Music Publishing (UK) Limited/
EMI Music Publishing Ltd

Lazarus
Bowie
RZO Music Limited

Love Yourself
Bieber/Blanco/Sheeran
Sony/ATV Music Publishing (UK) Limited/
Universal/MCA Music Limited

Take Me Home
Hector/Mac/Glynne/Tsang
BMG Rights Management (UK) Limited

What Do You Mean?
Boyd/Bieber/Levy
Universal/MCA Music Limited/Bug Music Ltd/
Warner/Chappell North America Limited

When We Were Young
Adkins/Jesso
Universal Music Publishing Limited/
Universal/MCA Music Limited

PUBLISHED BY
WISE PUBLICATIONS
14-15 BERNERS STREET, LONDON, W1T 3LJ, UK.

EXCLUSIVE DISTRIBUTORS:
MUSIC SALES LIMITED
DISTRIBUTION CENTRE, NEWMARKET ROAD, BURY ST EDMUNDS,
SUFFOLK, IP33 3YB, UK.
MUSIC SALES PTY LIMITED
LEVEL 4, LISGAR HOUSE, 30-32 CARRINGTON STREET,
SYDNEY, NSW 2000, AUSTRALIA.

ORDER NO. AM1011967
ISBN 978-1-78558-327-8
THIS BOOK © COPYRIGHT 2016 BY WISE PUBLICATIONS,
A DIVISION OF MUSIC SALES LIMITED.

PRINTED IN THE EU.

YOUR GUARANTEE OF QUALITY
AS PUBLISHERS, WE STRIVE TO PRODUCE EVERY BOOK TO THE HIGHEST
COMMERCIAL STANDARDS. THE MUSIC HAS BEEN FRESHLY ENGRAVED AND
THE BOOK HAS BEEN CAREFULLY DESIGNED TO MINIMISE AWKWARD PAGE
TURNS AND TO MAKE PLAYING FROM IT A REAL PLEASURE.
PARTICULAR CARE HAS BEEN GIVEN TO SPECIFYING ACID-FREE, NEUTRAL-
SIZED PAPER MADE FROM PULPS WHICH HAVE NOT BEEN ELEMENTAL
CHLORINE BLEACHED. THIS PULP IS FROM FARMED SUSTAINABLE FORESTS
AND WAS PRODUCED WITH SPECIAL REGARD FOR THE ENVIRONMENT.
THROUGHOUT, THE PRINTING AND BINDING HAVE BEEN PLANNED TO
ENSURE A STURDY, ATTRACTIVE PUBLICATION WHICH SHOULD GIVE YEARS
OF ENJOYMENT. IF YOUR COPY FAILS TO MEET OUR HIGH STANDARDS,
PLEASE INFORM US AND WE WILL GLADLY REPLACE IT.

WWW.MUSICSALES.COM

CHART HITS

VOLUME 2

Adventure Of A Lifetime

**Words & Music by Guy Berryman, Chris Martin, Jon Buckland, Will Champion,
Mikkel Eriksen & Tor Erik Hermansen**

Featuring a bright and snappy guitar riff, an anthemic chorus and an up-beat disco rhythm,
this lead single from Coldplay's seventh album garnered acclaim from critics and audiences alike.
The accompanying CGI music video follows a band of chimpanzees discovering their love of music.

**Hints & Tips: Begin by practising the opening bars until you feel secure with the quick-moving
semiquaver patterns in the right hand that are a key feature of the song.**

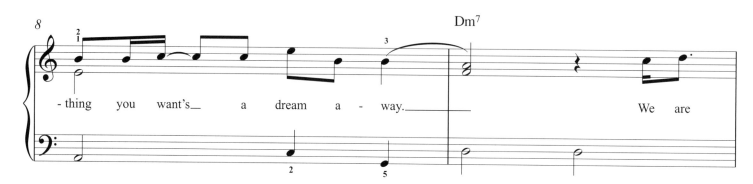

Black Magic

Words & Music by Edvard Erfjord, Henrik Michelsen, Camille Purcell & Edward Drewett

Little Mix deviated from their usual sound on this lead single, with its undeniably catchy hook,
'80s-infused disco beat and strong vocals. The song sold an incredible 600,000 copies in the UK,
being certified Platinum as a result.

**Hints & Tips: Note that the key signature contains two sharps: F♯ and C♯. Try not to put your thumb on
the black keys as this tends to change your hand position, making it hard to navigate the other keys.**

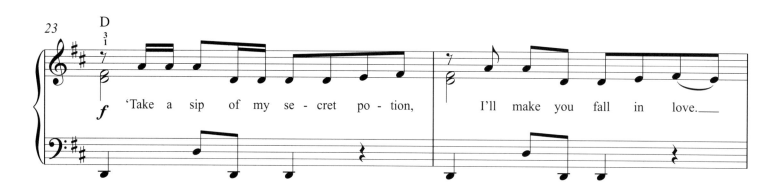

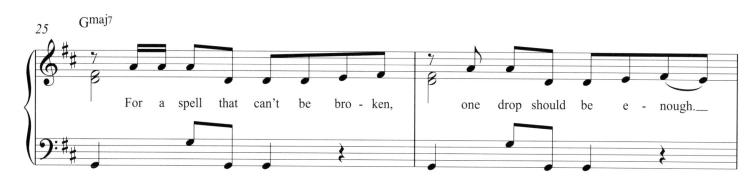

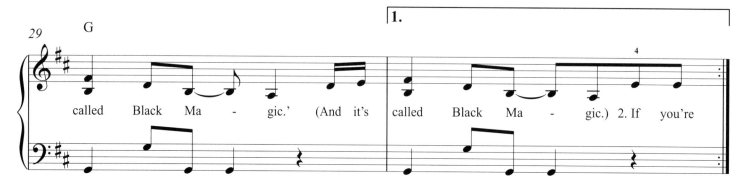

called Black Ma - gic.) Fall - ing in love, (Hey!)

fall - ing in love, I'm fall - ing in love, (Hey!)

fall - ing in love, (Hey!) fall - ing in love, (Hey!)

fall - ing in love, I'm fall - ing in love, (Hey!)

fall - ing in love. Ma - gic!

Hold Back The River

Words & Music by Iain Archer & James Bay

According to Bay, this song is about the feeling of being unable to see friends and family during a busy touring and recording schedule. After winning the Critics' Choice award at the Brits 2015 and seeing his album hit No. 1 in the UK Chart, his diary was so demanding that he welcomed the opportunity to finally see his loved ones.

Hints & Tips: Watch out at the start, as both hands are playing the same rhythm but different notes. Keep it steady and precise.

Eyes Shut

Words & Music by Oliver Thornton, Michael Goldsworthy & Resul Turkmen

This piano-based ballad has been described by Years & Years vocalist Olly Alexander as a personal torch song,
a melancholy tune that gives him inspiration when he's down. He had never intended for the song to appear on the album,
but fans and audiences responded well when it was performed live so they chose to include the song on their debut release.

Hints & Tips: Be conscious of the slight rhythmic difference between the notes on 'eyes shut' (bar 22)
and those on 'through them' (bars 23 and 24).

Hello

Words & Music by Greg Kurstin & Adele Adkins

As speculation about Adele's new music reached its peak, a cryptic advert appeared on UK TV which featured the first verse of this song. Adele had finally said "Hello" again to her fans after a three-year break from music, and the song was unveiled as the first single from her album *25*. The emotional ballad marked a stunning return for the 27-year-old, debuting at No. 1 in the UK Charts in October 2015.

Hints & Tips: Count the rhythms of all the tied notes carefully before you begin.
This rhythm is repeated throughout.

History

**Words & Music by Wayne Hector, John Ryan, Julian Bunetta,
Liam Payne, Louis Tomlinson & Edward Drewett**

This acoustic guitar ballad is a nostalgic look back at the rise and rise of One Direction.
Written by 1D's Liam and Louis, along with regular collaborators, the song is meant to be
their own version of a classic singalong like 'You've Got A Friend'.

Hints & Tips: Note the time signature: you will need to count in dotted crotchets rather than crotchets. Watch out for
the accidentals in the verse too!

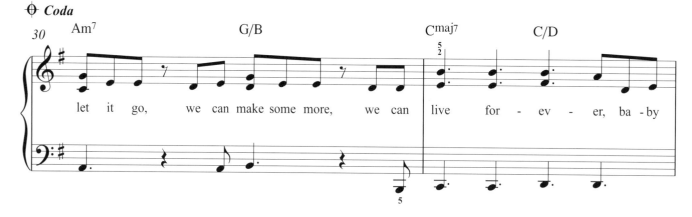

Hold My Hand

Words & Music by Ina Wroldsen, Jack Patterson, Jess Glynne & Janee Bennett

After topping the charts as the vocal talent behind Clean Bandit's biggest song, 'Rather Be', Jess Glynne took the top spot on her own with this anthem about someone being there for you in a tough time. Written with Jack Patterson from Clean Bandit and Glynne's friend Janee Bennett, Jess shows off her wide vocal range in a song that she says happened to come out sounding a little like Dolly Parton's hit '9 To 5'.

Hints & Tips: This is a fun song, so keep it light and bouncy. Make the most of the dynamic contrasts, starting off fairly quiet (*mp*) at the start and ending up loud (*f*) at the end.

25

Hymn For The Weekend

Words & Music by Guy Berryman, Mikkel Eriksen, Chris Martin, Jon Buckland, Will Champion,
Tor Erik Hermansen, Venor Timothy Yard, Scott Alan Zant & Marcus Tovar

The second single from Coldplay's seventh studio album, this song was originally conceived by lead singer Chris Martin as a 'party song' but, with the help of the rest of the band, the focus moved to the idea of having an angelic person in your life, which ultimately resulted in Beyoncé singing on the track.

Hints & Tips: The left hand plays thirds from bar 17 — be sure to bring your fingers down on the keys at the same time so the two notes sound exactly together.

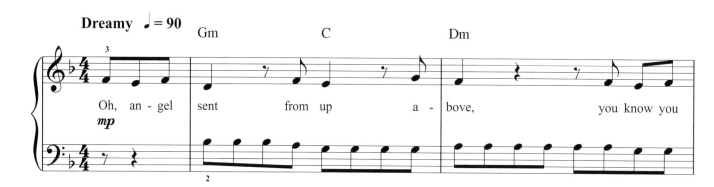

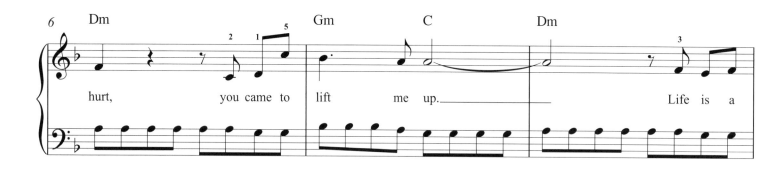

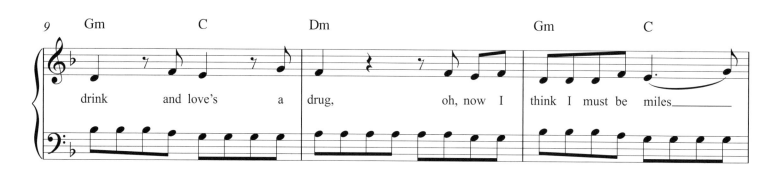

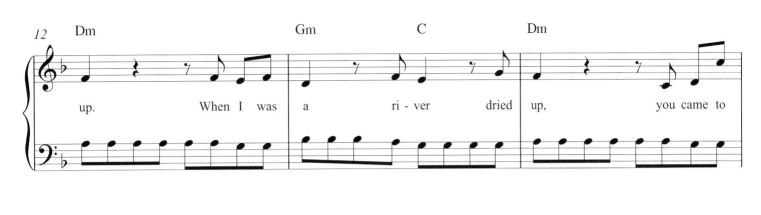

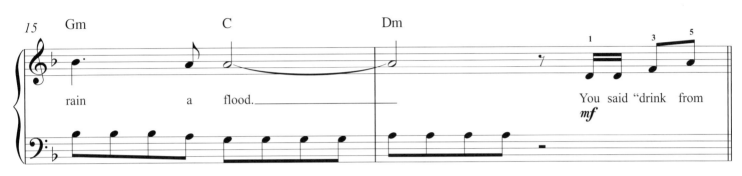

I Really Like You

Words & Music by Peter Svensson, Carly Rae Jepsen & Jacob Hindlin

Reportedly, when making plans for her third album *Emotion*, Carly Rae Jepsen's manager told her she couldn't release anything unless it was on the level of her biggest hit 'Call Me Maybe'. She then released this danceable number 'I Really Like You', whose chorus ensures it'll go down in pop history. The lyrics are about being in a relationship where it's just too soon to say "I love you".

Hints & Tips: Check the right-hand fingering all the way through. Practise any tricky sections, such as the start of the chorus in bar 17, on their own.

Oh,_____ did I say too much? I'm so in

my head when we're out - ta touch, out - ta touch!

I real - ly, real - ly, real - ly, real - ly, real - ly, real - ly like you.___

___ And I want you, do you want me, want me, do you want me too?

King

Words & Music by Andrew Smith, Oliver Thornton, Michael Goldsworthy, Resul Turkmen & Mark Ralph

The electropop band Years & Years won the prestigious BBC Sound of 2015 poll before releasing 'King', the fourth single from their debut album, *Communion*. Both single and album reached No. 1 in the UK Charts, making Years & Years a mainstay on festival stages throughout the summer. Singer Olly Alexander says that the song is about feeling like a king while in a relationship, yet knowing it has to end.

Hints & Tips: Practise this slowly at first then build up the speed when you're comfortable with playing hands together; this is quite an up-beat song and shouldn't drag.

Lay Me Down

Words & Music by James Napier, Sam Smith & Elvin Smith

'Lay Me Down' was the debut single from the debut album of British singing sensation Sam Smith. Smith chose to re-release the single after the success of his album, and also recorded a version with John Legend for 2015's Red Nose Day. A beautiful piano-based ballad about unrequited love, the song shows off the young singer's songwriting abilities as well as his stunning vocal range, moving through registers hitting every note perfectly.

Hints & Tips: There are some tricky chords in the left hand. Play them all through slowly at first, one after the other, taking time to make sure you've got your fingers in the right place before pressing the keys.

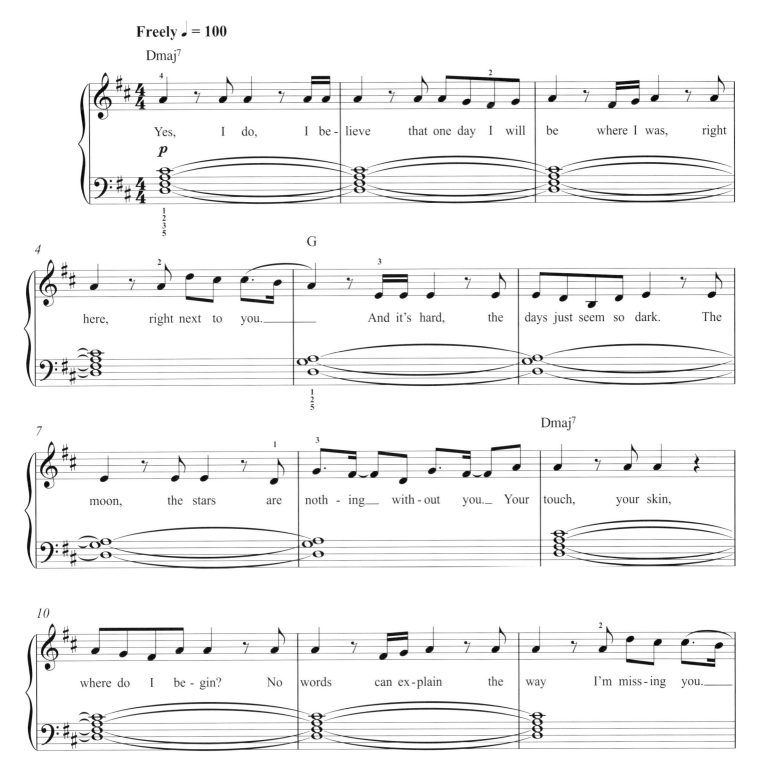

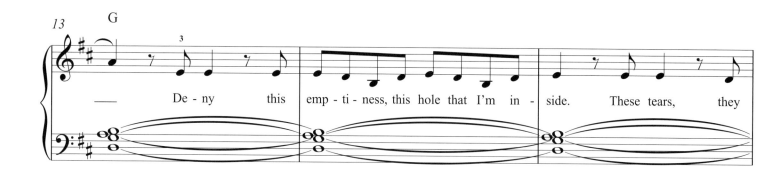

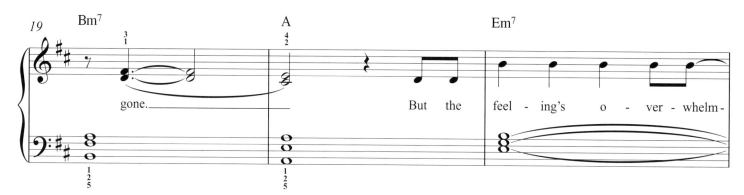

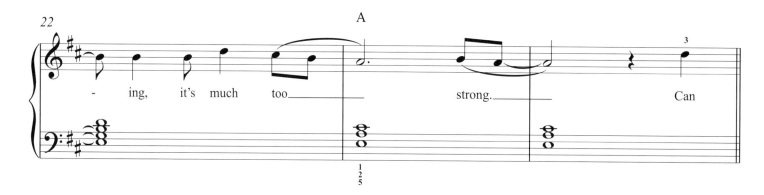

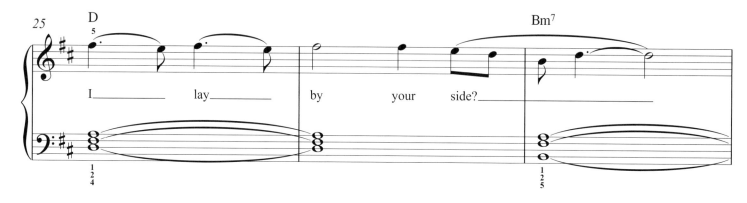

Lazarus

Words & Music by David Bowie

The second single from David Bowie's final album *Blackstar*, this song was released via a music video posted the day before the album was released, and just three days before Bowie passed away. The video sees Bowie wearing a bandage over his eyes and singing from a hospital bed. The day after Bowie's death, his longtime producer Tony Visconti suggested that the song and video formed a commentary on his own mortality.

Hints & Tips: There is a tricky left-hand riff that repeats throughout each verse. Practise this separately first so you get the hang of it, before adding in the right hand.

1. Look up here, I'm in hea - ven,
2. Look up here, man, I'm in dan - ger,

I've got scars that can't be seen.
I've got noth - ing left to lose.

I've got dra - ma, can't be
I'm so high, it makes my

What Do You Mean?

Words by Jason Boyd, Justin Bieber & Mason Levy
Music by Justin Bieber & Mason Levy

This tropical house-inspired tune was the lead single from Bieber's 2015 album *Purpose* and made him the fourth person to reach No. 1 in the UK with the same song on three different occasions. The eponymous question in this ode to ambiguity is posed a grand total of 28 times.

Hints & Tips: There are a lot of ledger lines in this piece. Ensure you are confident of the notes before you start so you can reach them quickly. The left hand should provide a steady pulse so keep the crotchets clear and on the beat.

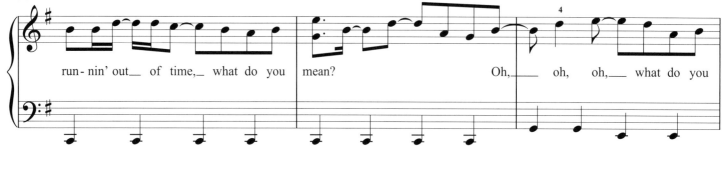

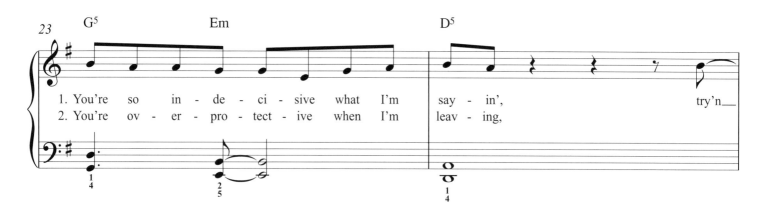

Love Yourself

Words & Music by Justin Bieber, Benny Blanco & Ed Sheeran

Justin Bieber's fantastically-catchy acoustic jam, with its simple chord progressions, laidback vocals and
sing-along chorus, captured a new generation of Beliebers in a movement away from his previous work.
The song was co-written by Ed Sheeran and notably knocked Bieber's own 'Sorry' from the top spot in the UK Chart,
making him the first person to do this since Elvis Presley.

**Hints & Tips: Clap through the right-hand rhythms first, making sure you count the semiquaver patterns
accurately and watch out for the single semiquavers.**

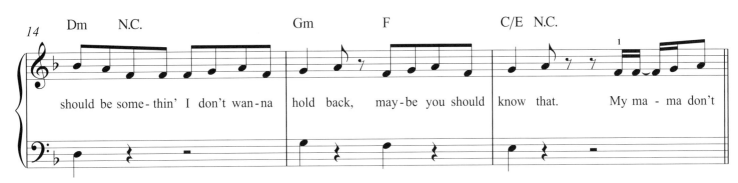

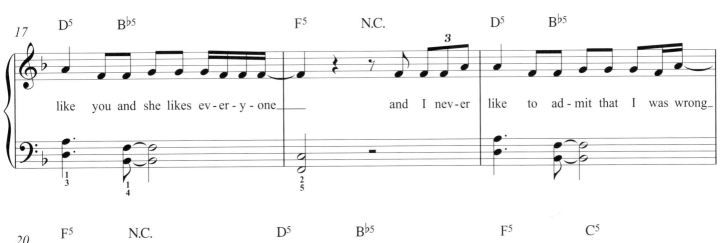

Take Me Home

Words & Music by Wayne Hector, Steve Mac, Jess Glynne & Nicholas Tsang

The UK's official 2015 Children in Need single appears on Jess Glynne's debut album. Speaking of the song, she said, "This is a song about the need to have someone who cares when you are at your most vulnerable... I hope it makes people realise that they should reach out to others at a time of need."

Hints & Tips: Practise the semiquaver passages from bar 26 in the right hand until confident. Make sure the notes are nice and even.

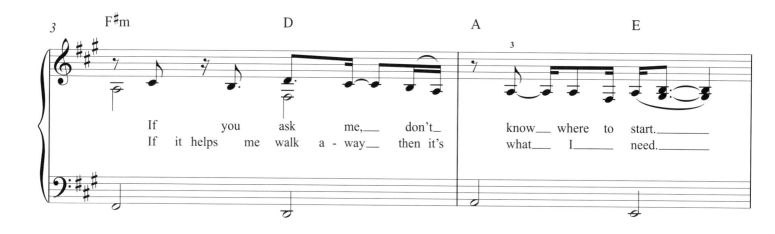

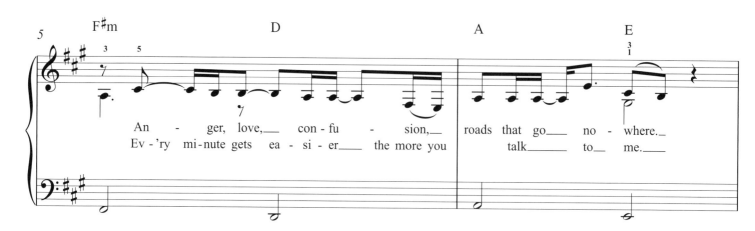

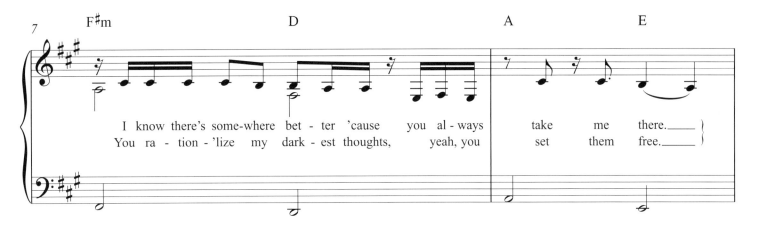

I know there's some-where bet - ter 'cause you al - ways take me there.____
You ra - tion - 'lize my dark - est thoughts, yeah, you set them free.____

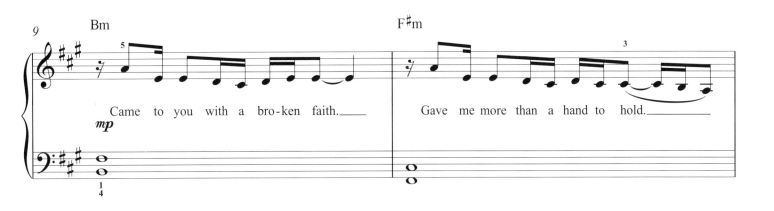

Came to you with a bro-ken faith.____ Gave me more than a hand to hold.____

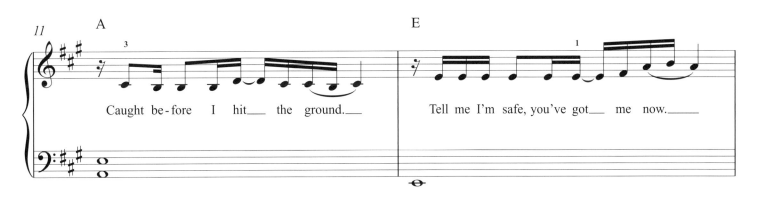

Caught be - fore I hit____ the ground.____ Tell me I'm safe, you've got____ me now.____

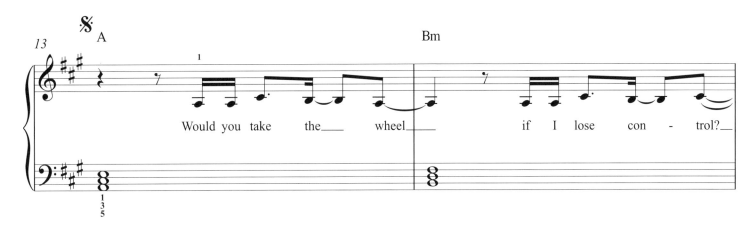

Would you take the____ wheel____ if I lose con - trol?

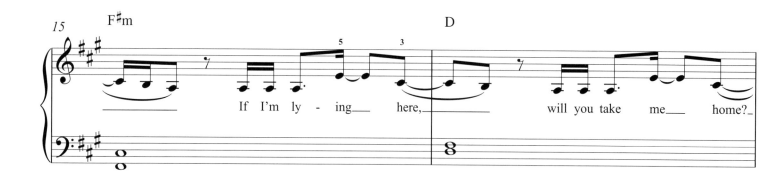

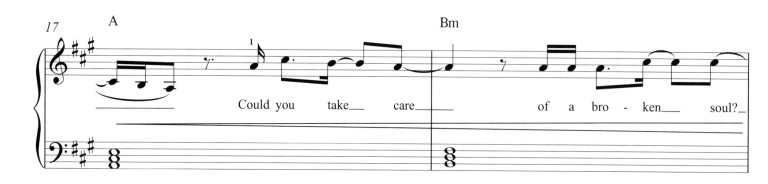

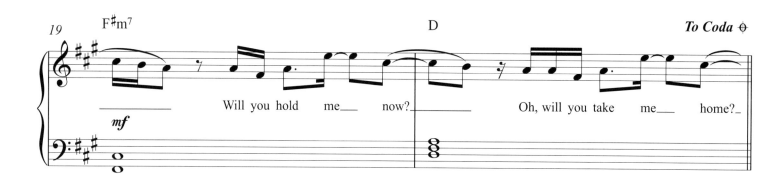

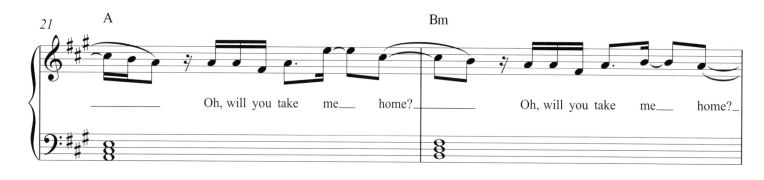

When We Were Young

Words & Music by Adele Adkins & Tobias Jesso

This song was reportedly composed by Adele and Tobias Jesso Jr. on a piano that used to belong to composer Philip Glass. Adele has stated that of all the songs on *25*, this one means the most to her because it's about spending time with old friends, reminiscing, and "feeling like you're 15 again".

Hints & Tips: The right hand goes quite low in this. Work out any of the ledger line notes you're not sure of and write them down in pencil; you can erase them when you're confident!

really easy piano

Collect the PLAYALONG series...

The *Really Easy Piano Playalong* series provides you with
easy piano arrangements of hit songs with a unique download card
that gives you demonstration and playalong tracks for each tune.

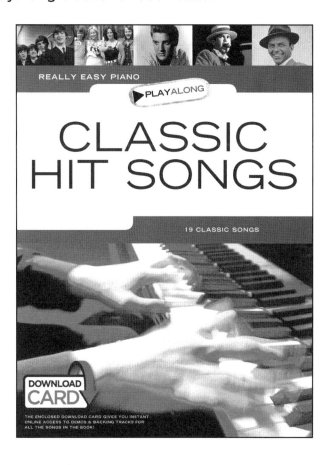

CHART HITS Volume 1

AM1010647

Best Song Ever One Direction
Dance With Me Tonight Olly Murs
Happy Pharrell Williams
Just Give Me A Reason P!nk
Just The Way You Are Bruno Mars
Let Her Go Passenger
Let It Go Idina Menzel
Pompeii Bastille
Roar Katy Perry
A Sky Full Of Stars Coldplay
Someone Like You Adele
Somewhere Only We Know Lily Allen
Stay Rihanna
A Thousand Years Christina Perri
Thinking Out Loud Ed Sheeran
We Are Never Ever Getting Back Together Taylor Swift
Wrecking Ball Cyrus, Miley

CLASSIC HIT SONGS

AM1010658

Ain't No Sunshine Bill Withers
All Shook Up Elvis Presley
Bridge Over Troubled Water Simon & Garfunkel
Can't Buy Me Love The Beatles
Downtown Petula Clark
Fields Of Gold Sting
The First Cut Is The Deepest Cat Stevens
Georgia On My Mind Ray Charles
Hallelujah Leonard Cohen
Have I Told You Lately Van Morrison
He Ain't Heavy, He's My Brother The Hollies
It Must Be Love Madness
Life On Mars? David Bowie
My Way Frank Sinatra
Rocket Man Elton John
Songbird Eva Cassidy
Somethin' Stupid Frank Sinatra, Nancy Sinatra
Waterloo Abba
What A Wonderful World Louis Armstrong

Just visit your local music shop and ask to see our
huge range of music in print. In case of dificulty, contact
marketing@musicsales.co.uk

HOW TO DOWNLOAD YOUR MUSIC TRACKS

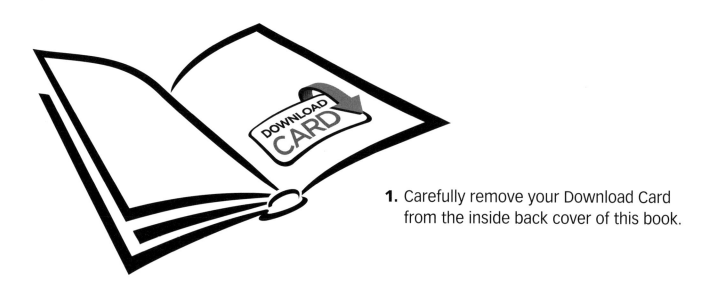

1. Carefully remove your Download Card from the inside back cover of this book.

2. On the back of the card is your unique access code. Enter this at www.musicsalesdownloads.com

TO REDEEM THIS CARD VISIT
www.musicsalesdownloads.com
ENTER ACCESS CODE:

XXXXXXXXXX

Download Cards are powered by Dropcards.
User must accept terms at dropcards.com/terms
which are adopted by The Music Sales Group.
Not redeemable for cash. Void where prohibited or restricted by law.

DCARD1006478

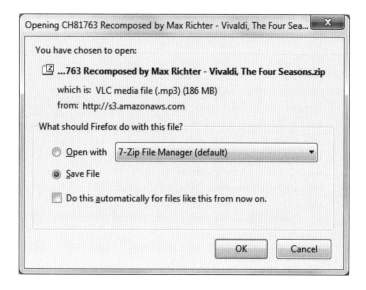

Opening CH81763 Recomposed by Max Richter - Vivaldi, The Four Sea...

You have chosen to open:

...763 Recomposed by Max Richter - Vivaldi, The Four Seasons.zip

which is: VLC media file (.mp3) (186 MB)

from: http://s3.amazonaws.com

What should Firefox do with this file?

Open with   7-Zip File Manager (default)

Save File

Do this automatically for files like this from now on.

OK   Cancel

3. Follow the instructions to save your files to your computer*. That's it!

*Appearance of download manager will vary depending upon operating system and web browser.
In case of difficulty when downloading files, please contact dropcards.com/help
Card missing? Please contact music@musicsales.co.uk